Pregnant

A Journey Into Motherhood

Kendra Fuller

Pregnant

A Journey Into Motherhood

Kendra Fuller

Railroad Street Press

Copyright (c) 2012 by Kendra Fuller

All rights reserved

Printed in the United States of America

Illustrated by Kendra Fuller

LIBRARY OF CONGRESS
CATALOGING-IN-PUBLICATION DATA
_____

Pregnant / Fuller

First Printing
1 2 3 4 5 6 7 8 9 10

ISBN 9781936711284

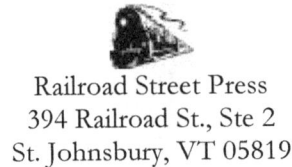

Railroad Street Press
394 Railroad St., Ste 2
St. Johnsbury, VT 05819

August 4th 2012
19 weeks 3 days

I'M GETTING THE NURSERY REDY

August 7th 2012

LAST NIGHT HE HAD HIS FIRST HICCUPS!
...SO CUTE

Hic Hic

August 14th 2012

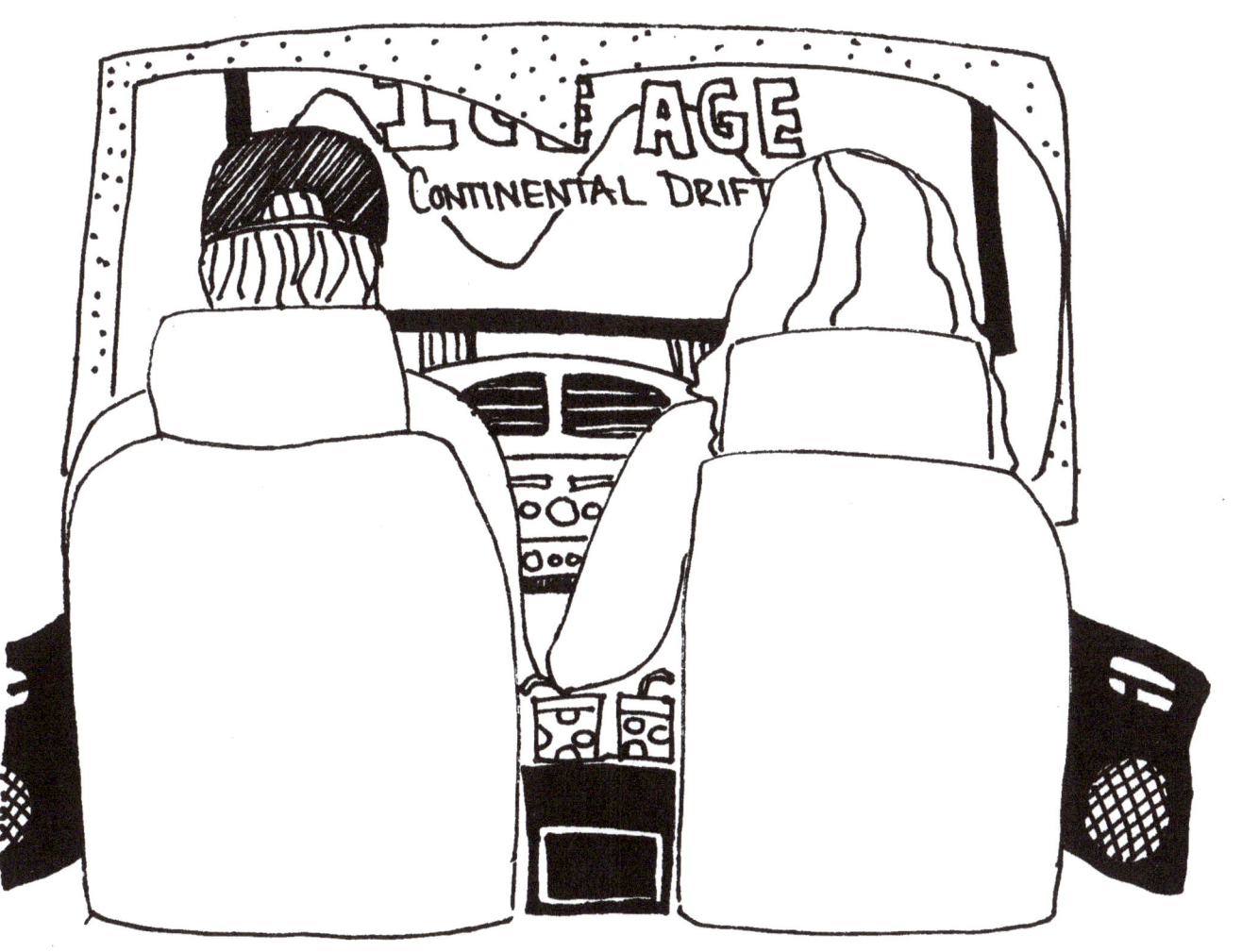

GRAMMY AND MIMI ARE SO EXCITED!

Mommy & Daddy went to the fair!

No rides for mommies... but we had fun!

August 23rd 2012

I FEEL SICK TODAY...

August 31st 2012

...AND TIRED...

WHEN I DRAW, MY HAND FALLS ASLEEP...

September 1st 2012

I CAN'T WAIT TO SHOW YOU OFF TO THE WORLD

SEPTEMBER 4TH 2012

DADDY MADE US A NICE BREAKFAST TODAY....

HAPPY BIRTHDAY TO MOMMY! 33 YEARS OLD

SEPTEMBER 10TH 2012

IF HEARTBURN MEANS WYATT'S GROWING HAIR, I THINK HE MIGHT LOOK LIKE THIS....

September 18th 2012
25 weeks 6 days

I WISH I COULD TURN INTO A BIG BEAR AND SLEEP UNTIL IT'S TIME

TO HAVE THE BABY...

SEPTEMBER 25TH 2012

BABY WYATT CAN KICK THE TV REMOTE OFF MY BELLY NOW!

September 26th 2012

I FEEL LIKE THE BABY IS IN MY CHEST I'M SO UNCOMFORTABLE

OCTOBER 18TH 2012

THE DOCTORS WANT ME TO HAVE THE BABY THREE WEEKS EARLY

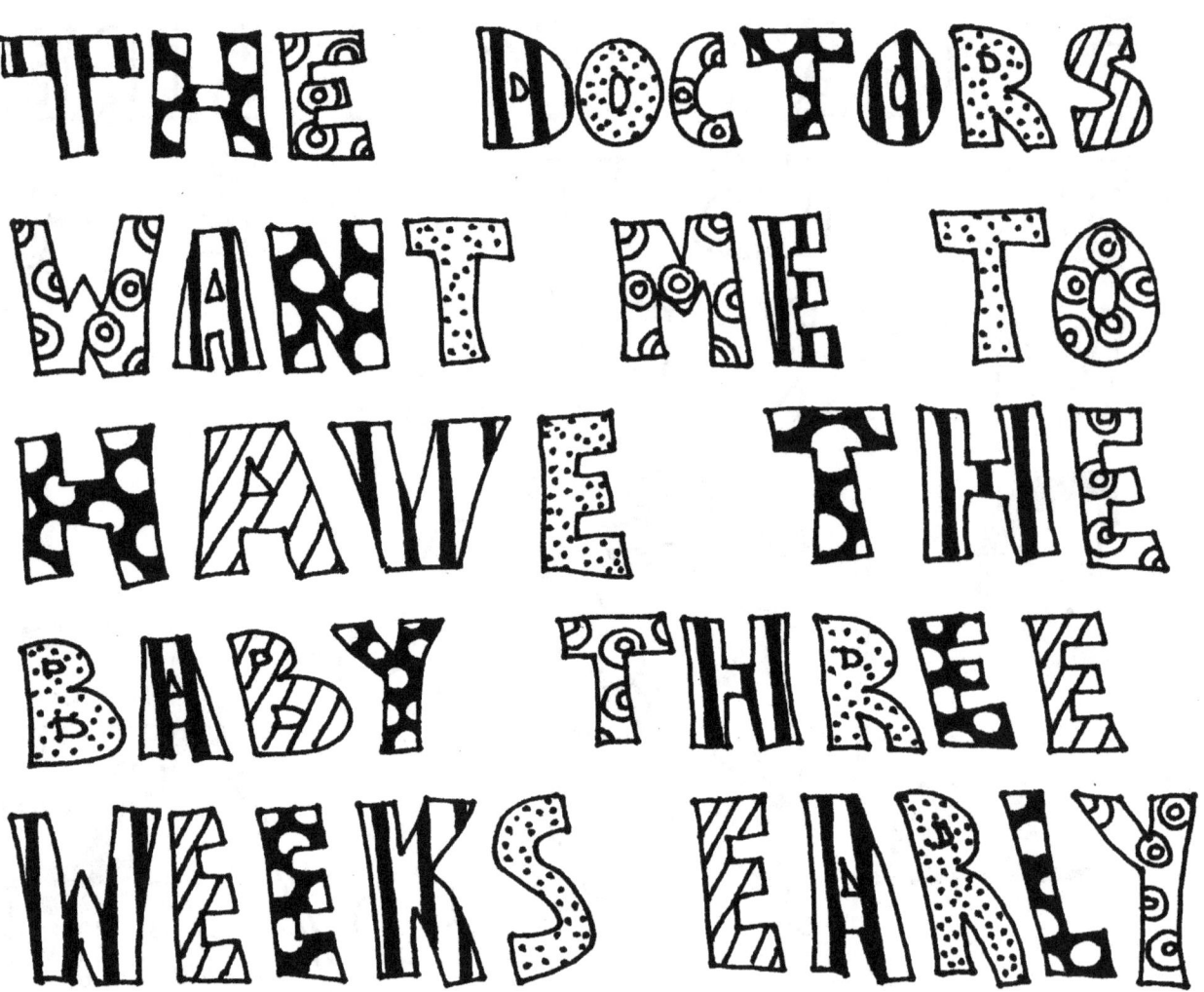

NOVEMBER 4TH 2012

THE DOCTOR SAYS THE BABY IS SO BIG, THAT I HAVE TO GET A C-SECTION!

I'M SO SCARED... NERVOUS... ANXIOUS... TIRED... EXCITED...

DECEMBER 6TH 2012

WHAT AN AMAZIN FEELING... TO BE A PARENT!

December 16th 2012

www.ingramcontent.com/pod-product-compliance
Lightning Source LLC
Chambersburg PA
CBHW081636040426
42449CB00014B/3342